HOME
AND
AWAY

POEMS
BY
IAN WISEMAN

Pottersfield Press
Lawrencetown Beach, Nova Scotia, Canada

Canadian Cataloguing in Publication Data

Wiseman, Ian

      Home and Away

      Poems
      ISBN 1-895900-27-1

I. Title.

PS8595.I816H6 1999   C811'.54   C99-950153-4
PR9199.3.W544H6 1999

Pottersfield Press gratefully acknowledges the ongoing support of the Nova Scotia Department of Education, Cultural Affairs Division, as well as the Canada Council for the Arts. We acknowledge the financial support of the Government of Canada through the Book Publishing Industry Development Program for our publishing activity.

Cover illustration: *Summer Interior* by Christopher Pratt. Used with the permission of the artist.

Printed in Canada

Pottersfield Press
83 Leslie Road
East Lawrencetown,
Nova Scotia, Canada, B2Z 1P8

THE CANADA COUNCIL | LE CONSEIL DES ARTS
FOR THE ARTS | DU CANADA
SINCE 1957 | DEPUIS 1957

FOR NANCY
AND EVELYN

(To those I have written about,
to those I have been unable to write about,
and to those who remember things differently,
my apologies.)

Acknowledgements

Earlier versions of some of these poems have been previously published in *Headlock, Pottersfield Portfolio* and *Staple*, and in *Newfoundland and Labrador Arts and Letters, Volume II*.

A tip of the hat to my parents, Rupert and Peggy Wiseman, for their help with the details of the Bay section; and to my friend, Jim Brokenshire, for his help with the City section.

Thank you to those who read parts of the manuscript and who made useful suggestions — Patrick Friesen, Sharon Gray, Jean McNeil and Nancy Robb. And thank you to those who tried to guide me along the path to publication — Ian Brown, Christina Hartling, Robert MacDonald, Harry Thurston, Miriam Toews and Susan Walker.

Thanks to my editor, Lesley Choyce, for having faith in the manuscript, for helping to strengthen it, and for his headlong energy in publishing it. Thanks to Peggy Amirault, who does the heavy lifting at Pottersfield Press. And a special thanks to Christopher Pratt for allowing us to use his painting, *Summer Interior*, to illustrate the cover.

Contents

AWAY

THE BAY

The edge of the world

passive
the beach emerges
submerges
the ocean washes the shore
push pull, a curve of froth

I prefer the cliff's
surf wreck and updraft
a catch in my breathing
a brutal dislocation of crust
the angular skirt of a continent

December hockey

We scatter and gather on a smooth miracle,
the work of a windless night.

When the puck
rolls near the unlocked end where the brook
circulates, a small child full of misplaced trust
retrieves it.

The ice is clear, revealing waist-
deep water with white air trapped in places,
and moves in waves, a boom and grumble
under the burden of too many skaters.

I can see my house, my mother, heartache
at the window as I make my own choices.

Chimney fire

We burn the stack of spruce and fir
that leans against the shed, split tinder,

dry enough to lift with fingertips
but streaked with hardened myrrh and gum.

Softwood leaves a stringy carbon rosin
welded to the mortar in the flue,

to rough surfaces in the chimney pot,
brittle when cold, sparkling with diamonds.

One night this sooty distillate erupts,
a terrible sucking roar, the masonry cracking,

a luminous blue gas loose in the attic
creeping on the brick.

New snow

maddened by freedom
her snout tossing the snow
the dog races near the trees

into the meadow I tramp
returning carefully, backwards
overprinting each footstep

Jacob lies on his back
gingerly crafting arcs
outlining a perfect angel

white patterns on a white field
already disappearing
as the snow continues to spiral

too dark to see the dog now
can't read what we have written
unaware that we are mortal

The schoolyard

The sons of miners strike the seed
of fishermen, the Catholic beats
the Anglican, the merchant's child

is ostracized. Permanent marks
scratched in the register,
stubborn small-town facts.

A simple education — learn
to recognize, accept the act,
and bully in one's turn.

Highway at night 1

Even the air has been burned.
>An immense nimbus above the trees,
>the blanket of carbon reaches down,
>flakes of soot like snow in our headlights.

The way ahead opens into fire
>running in valley and ditch, rivers
>that must have crossed the road somehow,
>twisters of flame, bursting branches.

Intent on home, my father drives.
>One sister mimics his tense silence,
>the other in hysterics, urgent, rigid,
>my mother shushing my smart-ass remarks.

Blackened sticks absorb the eerie glow.
>In time when the ash turns back to earth
>these will be good berry grounds.
>We'll snare rabbits and shoot partridge here.

Salmonier Pond

Knee deep in pond water
my fingers clamping line to rod
my eyes could be blind
for all they see.
I am of many minds
soccer, success, cities, sex
the normal Latin declension.

Behind me an English setter
resolutely of one mind
up to her belly in darkening cold
keeps an unwavering watch
not moving until a parr
we call them salmon peel
ripples my red-and-white bobber.

Meteorite

My father gave me a fragment
an unvaporized nugget of slag
a piece of an alien firmament
glazed on one face, with small bubble marks
iron transformed in a violent
time and somehow propelled through the dark.

A man in a campus laboratory
(as I'm thinking, what does *he* know?)
says he'll only talk probability
ship's ballast, Welsh smelter stone
so to me the rock stays a mystery
and my questions unanswered, postponed.

Old Man's Beard

Everyone must live someplace.
The simple moss hangs from the spruce
but takes nothing from it —

so independent, so light,
moved by wind,
unmoved by wind.

What kind of air is this,
carrying enough moisture and nutrients
to sustain life?

Slender green and white tendrils —
root, stem, flower, leaf,
all look the same.

Sometimes the little brown birds
steal some to soften a nest.
Everyone must live someplace.

Francis

Francis is sitting on the wharf
watching us throw ore in the harbor,
chalky fluorspar, purple and red crystals,

spilled by the trucks, the conveyor belts,
the men who load the rusty boats.
I hadn't noticed him getting old.

I hadn't noticed his doleful face,
a carapace slowly hardening to stone,
flesh separating into the same chalk,

the same angry purples and reds.
Looking up through his coarse eyebrows
now he's watching a funeral procession,

a line of low beams approaching,
crawling along the lower road, a precursor,
his stroke coming faster than his birthday.

The line

Loner, self-contained, taciturn:
I'll fight these genes my whole life.
He likes his own company, my sisters say.

I walk out on the headland
dreamy, heedless, lonely.
Gulls with fixed wings float on air currents.

Over bare rock down to the tideline,
not the lower one
marked by rotting kelp and barnacle life,

but the upper one, on the granite stripped
by storm flush, ice field, gravity.
You have to look carefully.

Below: small blue shells come and go.
Above: loose stones and stone-colored lichens,
high enough to stay for centuries,

and a few larger shells, half-moon
pieces of sea urchins,
rusty crabs, broken, eaten alive by gulls.

The gulls dive and scream as sun-blind
I descend, isolated, tremors
in my neural tunnels, no stones to throw.

I think my mind may be like this:
I live high, near the top, above
the zone that has the screaming.

Mrs. Burton

Still sunny at sixty, she laughs
down by the government wharf —
a daisy nests behind one ear,
a terrier sniffs her naked shin.
Embracing a man's quiet hand,
linked and fused, husband and wife,
she views his face, his engraved husk.
He scans the horizon, then the surf.

Her face can soften into dough.
I've seen the tears through pleated veil.
They buried young her youngest son,
a boy with deference, discipline,
a friend of mine, a teammate, too,
whose midfield play had satin style.
A winter death, leukemia.

She cannot write or read as such.
She mocks the sound of words I know
— wisdom, benevolence, *élan* —
and (here's the lie of literacy)
in none of these am I her match.

Shoal Cove and Salt Cove

I grew up near two beaches
a headland in between.

Shoal Cove has fine sand
the universal kind
continually recoining itself
new decimals pitched ashore
the old diminished to mud
or dust. It's not as blond
as Caribbean powder
and not as bright —
dull and cold and sullen
just below the surface
on even the sunniest days.

Salt Cove has rounded stones
fist-sized knobs and buns
once inner-planet magma
since eroded by glaciers
and rolled by hurricane tides.
Some are fine-grained eggs
browns and grays that turn dark
when I wet them.
Others are coarser granites
off-whites and pinks
some spangled with mica
or marked with pocks and veins.
When I bounce them, they chime
the plink and clack of pool balls
and rumble in small avalanches.

Two residues, two congregations
so close and so unmixed
like Protestants and Catholics.

June fog

the lamp-post keeps you upright
above us two shapely rings
of greenish blue create
a corona in textured air
as soft as your mouth
I see an achromatic fence an outline
of primitive rails four feet away
beyond that nothing
your father's invisible pasture

miners become careless
women miscarry
the soccer team never loses
horses run in the street

A miner's funeral

Murmuring with the mourners
     ignoring the crunch of soil
diggers cover the gilded wood
     one more cellar to parcel the hill
a grown man who used to panic
     when he couldn't find his breath.

Dust orbits the headframe
     industry, money, modern time
work, fatigue, death
     the big world and the little one.
No, no, don't close it.
     Build us a hospital instead.

Everybody knows

Salter is assured   confident with the ball
his field instincts incandescent   seeing things
trusted by the other boys.   Girls he answers
the same   not eager, not bragging, responding
in a relaxed way   to dances and kisses.
Not really handsome   but somehow elected
to the grand society.   Descended gods.
Mysterious   and yet everybody knows.

Salter seems immune now   but one transgression
opens the laneway   to shadowy exile
bootless, uninvited, lost.   Few are favored
and each turn is brief.   The parents are shut off
from this magic   except the woman who's kept
her waistline   and the man who has some money.

Notre Dame Bay

the boat launcher hugs himself
hunches his back
probably wishes he'd brought an overcoat

out on the bay an active traffic in icebergs
sails in full trim
keels scratching the seabed

the water from the brook
crystallizes as it strikes the salt
a confusion of seasons

Lives lived forever

Loping home   under solid clouds
east a pale filament   four A.M. outline
black hills   tenuous diagram of street lamps
a few houses brightening   around the harbor.
Here's one curtains apart   spilling a trapezoid
of yellow light in the lane.   Neil Molloy senior
looks at the window   expressionless
viewing his reflection?   divining the weather?
Mrs. Molloy at the stove   her back to him.
He'll be maneuvering his skiff   carrying nets
carefully folded   half-cylinder traps for lobster
she if she's energetic   weeding the vegetables
lives lived forever.   I step in a puddle
curse   trying to skirt that pool of light.

Chambers Cove

Pay attention   to one thing at a time
my grandfather likes to say   but I've cycled
to the end of the track   hiked along the cliffs
descended past nests and vexed gulls   to this cove
thinking the whole time   of something else
thinking of one solid fact   you   the resist
and yield of you   advancing beside me.
Clouds darken the air and cool it.   We tent
some logs in a pyramid   soon honeycombed
with smoke that balances for a moment   then wavers
up through the rising decibels   of frantic birds.
I check the grooved sand   where I dragged the heavy
driftwood past the ghost ship   here since the war
looking for ammunition   to intensify the fireworks.

Evening

vesper bells
the baitman is drunk
paralysing his wife

the sun comes up
and burns
and sets

but the setting part
that's just *naiveté*
vanity, narrative

the truth is
the *earth* turns away
we make our own dark

Hagdowns

First the *pop-pop-pop* of the inboard
as we follow the edge of the fog bank.

Seabirds we call hagdowns migrate south
along the horizon, just above the waves,

beneath human radar. Birds moving,
skiff moving, walls of water in between.

Balancing against the roll and pitch and yaw,
we slipslide on the hills and hollows.

Then the *pop-pop-pop* of the shotguns,
the explosions soft, diffused in infinite air.

Brackish water

Slack water musty murky half a mile wide
flat almost lifeless although something

has pushed a cloud of yeast onshore
and the pilings are fringed with algae.

Alex can go up on the river's slow pulse
or the other way out on the exhaling bay.

Please God let him make that first step
then momentum may keep him going.

Cape Chapeau Rouge

For seventeen years I've been looking
    at this dead volcano, broad shouldered,
truncated neck where the cone once stood,
    long extinguished flame half-seen
through the gloomiest fog. Up through
    the curling damp I have climbed
until I sat on the summit in clear air,
    a layer of real clouds higher up.

On bright days everyone can see it —
    fishermen returning with empty boats,
miners risen from exhausted tunnels,
    defeated women hanging out clothes.
The soccer players aim for it
    when they're attacking the south goal.

THE CITY

Major events

Happy to breathe moving air   I left the newsroom
silent unpopulated   a pocket of toxic aromas
astringent ink   torpor of melted lead
ferment of dry rot   sear and scour of ammonia.

Now there are tornadoes   angry centrifuges
around the publisher   and the news editor
lips papery with irritation   *One person has to stay*
at all times   in case of major events.

I've seen the inert driver   the accordioned door
the spilled thermos of soup   the woman's eyes
seeing what I see   in the back two small children
necks and limbs   at uncorrectable angles.

I first saw that wreck   thirty years ago.
Until today   I couldn't write the story.

The White Fleet

A cold truth, a night truth, stirs on the docks—
the air blows acrid, keen, raw.

We stop kicking the empty can,
quicken our steps
and look for a place to urinate.

The Portuguese fleet is in port
running from tomorrow's thunder.

Laughing nervously, two prostitutes pass
and leave a faint smell of semen,
perhaps attached to hair or sleeve.

Skittish, rash, but somehow honest
and constant — that's how the docks are.

The Tudor Inn
(for J.B.)

The waitress expertly lowers her tray,
untouched by the churn and swirl —
another round, long past closing time.
Jesus, they're smoking dope in the corner.

      Jack's been tasting his own stimulants —
      a perfect, dapper after-hours host,
      mustache in the microphone again,
      introducing the boys for the third time.

The Ralph Walker Orchestra, starring
Ralph himself on piano, with guitar, a couple
of horns, the dancers pouncing on the tempo,
heaving, jiving, bumping our table.

      Jack is handling the door now,
      six or eight of us huddled in the backfield.
      He looses the deadbolt, takes a quick peek
      before shushing us into the silent cold.

Your uncle's hammock

your uncle's hammock
      back country cabin
face down and tanning
      knitted mesh bedsling
bark peeling birch and a tall rusty pine

silhouette shadow
      cooling my shoulder
down through the netting
      tempered with tension
sunblocking cream falls on sandal and sand

midsummer heatwave
      afternoon sunset
vertigo stillness
      heart knocking eardrums
I have to remember I have to forget

Washington, 1969

(for H.D.)

The vibrating sputter stops.　　　　The Pontiac's
owner wakes　　　and finds himself five or six hours
farther north.　　　*We* last slept back in New Orleans.

There's nothing east of Maine　　　he keeps telling us
and I've stopped arguing.　　　He's off-course now but
unvexed　　　on schedule for a Boston funeral.

Police protect Nixon's sleep　　　and Abe Lincoln
the patriarch　　　looks out on the rest of us
night tourists　　　winos sprawling on the dark grass
homosexuals　　　prowling the public toilets.

At dawn we cross the Potomac and　　　can this
be true?　　　wash our unshaven faces inside
the Pentagon.　　　Hitchhiking in Maine that night
I lean on a pole and sleep　　　still going east.

Great Northern Peninsula
(for S.G.)

Wizened   not much taller than me
the trees are done in   by salt and sand
a strip of underfed scrub
between the road   and the Gulf.

Claiming the path at six paces
a lynx
immobile, stubby tail erect.

Since I've grown up   I've never camped
except with women   except for sex.
There, I've said it.
I prefer central heating   urban travel
being pampered.

Remarkable ears
pointed Star Trek ears with dark tips
one badly notched and scarred.

We pitched our tents on the beach   a mistake
the wind and sand   abrade the waterproofing.
One tent for me   and the woman I live with
the other for an earlier love
and her boyfriend   who's building the fire.

Leg muscles shivering
he stirs his nostrils
perhaps smelling my fear.

The Sixties came late   to Newfoundland
'67 to '73
maybe it was the same   everywhere.
Before that   boys believed in fraternity
barbershop harmony   authority
and girls   masturbated those boys
or refused to.
                    Today the girls bravely, blindly
suffer the pill   toxic creams   crippling devices
— the way can become the end —
sexual diseases are scarce
and *Cosmo*   keeps promoting the orgasm.

      Eyes never leaving mine the lynx
      vanishes in the undergrowth.
      My penis has shrivelled to a prune.

August on the docks

boys on their bikes where the asphalt spreads out
screaming and laughing and fooling around
dropping their wrappers and talking in curses
        a scraped arm   blood on the ground

one of them speaking the other one silent
old men with hats are defying the breeze
words blowing sideways and lifting in air now
        aggrieved tone   all I can hear

gold in his teeth and a rip in his jeans
a Portuguese sailor is kicking a football
and follows it into the bilge of the sea
        I wouldn't   if I were you

Logy Bay

Atop the poorly lit slipway   the winch
hitches and freewheels
           can't pull the load

a drowned shark   wrapped partly in tatters
of cod trap
        towed in by scientists.

Two men chop the shark   crunching through
coarse skin
        rubbery fibrous cartilage

and inside   organs soft gristle no bones
a legendary maw
          once home to hunger.

The way I am

Running just offshore the Labrador Current,
Calvinist in its nordic marrow,
coursing across the fishing grounds,

a city of ships bobbing above,
meets an opposing rush,
the Gulf Stream's *carnaval*, big-lipped fish

who'll never make it home again
gliding in its midway. One ocean over, *El Niño*,
softening my winter. Why has no easy answer.

I could blame my parents, their genes, hard times,
or further back their parents, early modernism,
the church, the school, pop culture.

The currents never stop, endless stamina, flowing
faster than I can walk. I know
the force, the laws of motion, the shadows

of submerged mountains, but what hidden hand
lifts them as vapor toward the sun,
great shafts that charge the air I breathe?

Restless

Call me when
you're in a good mood again.
I stay silent watching

a great-circle jet trail
the true line corrupting
decay abruptly while

out on the water a sail
filled with angled tension
turns impossibly into the wind.

Things surprise me
the ease of endings
sweet beer, red pubic hair.

East End Club

Blue particles in backlit smoke,
     a filterless cigarette
burning perilously close to his lip,
     rheumy eyes welling,
Bull bends over the slab
     — *Nine ball in the corner* —
and rams the shot passionately,
     snap of contact,
cueball curving, spinning in reverse,
     bringing a grin —
he can hit a second stroke
     without walking around the green.

The patrons are neutral, friendly;
     fights are rare.
They call me *The Newsman*
     and a few say it
enviously, a deliverance
     their children can pray for.

Women are forbidden
     or maybe they don't bother —
the rules are changing.
     The bartender is a woman,
Carmen, serving us
     stubby brown bottles,
Jockey Club or Dominion Ale,
     washing our scratched glasses,
and just before closing time
     showing off a few shots of her own.

Mike and Reg
(in memory)

Scabbed and scarred from their daily jags,
performing small dramas,
charming Reg on harmonica, little Mike dancing
a frail jig,
spelling words backwards —
E-T-T-E-R-A-G-I-C.

The winter of '71 they slept in our porch
on Bonaventure
and the morning aroma that led to their banishment
said sometimes the living room.
Slap and moan in the bathroom one night,
intramural extras.

Sampling marijuana with us, they agreed with me —
it leaves you stupid.
For this I've seen guys in jail,
Mike said,
but we won't tell.
I don't believe they ever did.

Boats

a rolling swell smooths
      a thick glaze of water
            over the rocks
we bump the cliff
      on the backwash seaweed
            floating beside us

tipping up the outboard
      we run the inflatable
            slanting up the strand
a gangly grey chick
      confined to the island
            pretends to be a stone

breaking the horizon
      the beautiful sailboats
            narcissistic
self-contained
      won't go ashore
            until they're home

Birthday

A sharp sensation wakes me.
I am a vase for a bouquet
of thin-stemmed field flowers —

a white daisy, a yellow buttercup,
a blue flower I can't name —
and now I'm a candlestick,

silver spun on rapture's lathe,
containing a slight festive candle
lit from a Holiday Inn matchbook.

Happy birthday, you grin.
How does it feel?
                   To be 22?
I blow out the tiny flame.

St. Clare's Mercy Hospital

Hey
> *I know you.*
You used to live
> > *in by the mine.*
Get me out of here.

The man we used to call Hogan,
Hogan no more.
Dark sockets, eyes in narcosis,
the blacks gasping for light,
blasted open, the browns flattened,
deflated, pinched.

Everything has a greenish glow,
a thin neon
tainted by nauseating ether.
Green concrete blocks hold in
the echo-echo of garbled doctor-calls.

I play pool with Darby,
my buddy. Laughing, talkative,
he sounds okay. Damp air
has warped and wrinkled the table
under the felt
and the balls as they slow
wobble and take unexpected sideslips.

I'll be out soon. I have to
stop
> *drinking,*
eat three meals a day.

Without anybody hitting it the red ball,
the three,
starts rolling again.

Waterford River

I dawdle longer than I should
to watch this dirty river sludge
running through the frozen city —

water flowing over, under,
an icy shelf at the river's edge.
The downstream side of a rusty cart

holds a perfect curve in water,
cold and thick and hypnotizing,
standing still. My mind is moving.

My forehead's burning in the wind.
Somehow damaged, thrown off-centre,
a wino with a listing canter

breaks the skins of gutter puddles,
heading for The Salvation Army,
a meal, a bed, autumn's end.

Northwest River, Labrador
(for N.M.)

Where are the gallant dogs, the blood
and bastardy of shepherd and husky
and wolf, that chased us yesterday?

No sound in the crystal air, no sign
on the white ground, crusted and stark.
The cameraman touches the brake

as the road curves into a mound of fur,
frozen corpses, each with the clotted
circular bite and spread stain of a bullet.

We have our own schedule, a deadline,
a documentary to complete —
no time to contemplate this mystery.

Red Cliff
(for D.M.)

rock tears metal
        darkness covers rock
                metal falls through darkness
I hear my name mixed with a distant splash

on the bruising cliffside
        my fingernails are hurting
as slowly I release my frozen breath

why would a man of judgement
        jump back inside the chamber
to straighten up those rolling, rattling wheels

a few things still remain
        insurance money, memory
this chill returning to my lower back

The mirror
(for E.D.)

Where can I collect the pieces to compose a face?
Calm unstirred surface, a topography of insouciance,
saying, look at this terrain.
                         The bathroom mirror calls
for some inner general to rally the troops from their tents
and march them forward in unchallengeable columns.

When will I find the time to construct enduring legs?
Regimented back sitting on an underframe of permanence,
square shoulders that stay square.
                         I seem asymmetric,
waving an invisible baton, one arm tight and out of balance,

other parts inappropriate, unstrung, a breakdown of order.

How, with these resources, can I orchestrate an attitude?
Gaiety, dignity at least, maybe even confidence,
a technical *tour de force*.
                         My demeanor is sour,
full of curdle, asocial black tones and dissonance,
gravity plucking bluenotes, the bottom of melancholy.

Which elements do I need to invent a voice?
Warm tones, vibrating vowels, crunchy consonants,
like a British comic actor.
                         I run the water,
hear my scratchy, deadened whisper try for resonance —
I'd straighten up, and change, if you would stay.

Prevailing winds

Some winds seethe with hazard   that day
the school door exploded   my hand
in the handle   flung me across the drive.
My mother dreamed   of murderous storms
me on my parka   sailing out the harbor.
Some winds can be subtle.   I barely felt the air
on my creeping prickling neck   the cheer
for my lucky first goal   the sigh of a girl saying *No*
the tousle of a teacher saying *Yes*.   Accidents
would deflect me   coincidence human breath.
These days I find tailwinds   or slipstreams
behind confident masters   meagre exertion
minimal friction.   Friends   careers   cities
choose me   and not the other way around.

Away

January night

Sleep is lost
to the peal and clap
of aluminum siding
contracting in the cold,

arid two-by-sixes
detonating, twisting
back into their natural
arboreal forms,

some staccato gunfire
from the radiator pipes,
the pedal and rumble
of trembling water.

I go to the window.
The pre-metric thermometer
says twenty below.

Outside, the mirror moon
is small and hard,
reflecting some light,

no warmth.

The missile

The crow walks on a whisker of curb,
beak open in a silent war cry,
wings spread
on the bank of currents from workweek cars.

Exhaust coughs into the air,
an abstract blue over the waxen plumage
shellacked with winter oils,
a sparkle on the blackest black.

He takes what he can from the frozen street —
today it's road salt.
As hard as I can I throw my apple core.
(Poets know crows.)

March crossing
(for R.C.)

the claustrophobic porthole
heavy salt-grimed glass
reinforcing bars
tiny impassable tunnel to freedom
is worse than a solid wall
       the moon looks full or close
       shining on a field of ice

we're travelling astern
our propellers screwing floes to pans
slowly widening the black fractures
on a flattened sea
       the wind can't reach the water
       screened it falters into languor

the sounds of the mechanical strain
and the diesel-driven friction
trigger a nightmare my grandfather gave me
       a prairie of ice the only shore
       a ship at night on fire

Long distance

I know they do something to the voice
that deadens the highs and lows. They translate it
into electricity
and microseconds later relay it as an echo,
a hollow mimicry of speech.
They have to do this.
Sound is too slow, the thunder far behind the spark,
almost part of something else.

The translators change the message, too,
and the person across the span
can't always catch
what I mean to say. My mother
has been suffering in a hospital
but she sounds more fretful
about me
than I do about her.

St. John's

The spice of taxi air, a crucifix
under the mirror, midnight
on the dashboard. My second ear pops,
re-pressurizing for sea level.

Veering rivulets on the glass,
a smear of sleepy houses.
Portugal Cove Road seems Protestant,
sober, suburban, diagonal.
Rawlin's Cross is apocalyptic,
a steep hill, clashing intersections,
oldtime Pentacostal, now subdued.
Queen's Road feels quite Catholic,
blessed by the blur of the Basilica,
sanctioned by squat City Hall
— is Dorothy Wyatt still the mayor? —
then a tall hotel where clapboard
used to warm crooked homes.

I open the drapes at seven, see
my first daylight, and the Southside Hills,
formed by unknowable forces,
grip my gut and tell me I'm home.

Two glimpses

startled by the car door
the heron beats the water to shards
laboring
dripping stilts lifting behind

Nancy swings her legs out
fully formed calves
incurving thighs

she's full of herons
wants to write a book
wants my thoughts

nowhere

Outside the hubbub

Adjusting her shoulder-strap
                        she tells me her childhood
her father   the detective   with the R.C.M.P. —
his spy games, his photos.
                    I open a window
disturbing a spider's web   chasing my thought.

Those short-haired men
                    on the fringes of protests
outside the hubbub   with their telephoto lenses?
Perhaps he's the one
                who threatened our printer
(the manifesto edition)   tried to veto my press card.

Admiring the campus
                that landscape of privilege
I know I'm her favorite   his daughter   my student.
He hates the new clemency
                 his whimsical snapshots

his years incognito   all come to nought.

Cakewalk

Tea steam and rain clouds frame our reserve,
a loaded emotional holdback

over eggs and toast. Still in my housecoat,
reading at the counter, I hear you

telegraph forgiveness, breathe my name.
I rip the box top off the tea bags,

use it as a bookmark and, watching
the mirror, cakewalk down the hall.

Highway at night 2

the diamonds in the middle distance
arrive like flares
melodramatic pictures
the heraldry of unnamed prophets
painted starkly, black on yellow
deer crossing, crooked road, falling rock

the baby beside me translates my face
and responds in a perfect Esperanto
the tone, the expression
the eyes
even the dog is talking
and surely her memory
is scored with cave-drawings, too

language without words

Inside and out

Christmas trees in the city
have a formal look
like Lombardy poplars or Italian cypresses,
cigar-shaped,
trussed up to make space in the truck.

It takes a day for the limbs
to relax. We wait
— I don't know why —
to load the tips with electricity and angels,
with the longings of the solstice,
to pull them out of balance again.

Already deep in their winter death,
the birch and maple
have acquiesced. The rhododendrons
don't want to be out there,
shrivelled and black, undeserving
of *evergreen*. The only color in the yard,
the junipers and spruce look fine,
shouldering the snow.

Up to no good

Now:
arc of the crow
quiet *krraaawt*
almost contrite
in the milky calm
of early dawn

up to no good

and now:
chased with such shrieking
damned and decried
by a cackle of grackles

spring.

Istanbul, 1989

my daughter is three
soon four
her crest has yet to darken
today her irises look freshwater blue
a trick of the Bosphorus perhaps

on the dock near the fish market
a woman in a shawl touches her cheek
lifts her quickly
I imagine the worst
violence abduction
Islamic revenge for some age-worn grievance

I seize her back gracelessly
the unguarded woman staggers
bends down
offers the child a flower
then in tears she rights herself

and in faltering unfinished English says
she has colored eyes

Snakes and Ladders

Relaxation for me   a contest for her
leaning over the cardboard
                              inclined neck

knuckles gripping dice.   It's hard to imagine
a child
              needing more instruction in life

the sudden sadness   and unexpected setback
of sliding down a snake
                      the lesson that a bend

in the road   is not the end of the road
and the one big lie
                      the ease of climbing ladders.

The rules don't teach us   how to ascend
how to practise the drill
                      to lose our fear of heights.

Victims of Shostakovich

Not my taste, this gloomy music.

Ceasefire at the symphony. The closing phrase
still colors my ears,
now adjusting to two gentlemen
cradling intermission drinks.

Mine, either. The grieving of stick figures.

Their neckties are a daring red.
They've seen me
and dismissed me,
a solitary man in a torn sweatshirt, leaning
against the architect's conceit, a false wall
with inlaid stones,
listening.

Before the modern
there was a romance by Mozart
and a man in front of me was audibly humming
that old familiar tune.

Sidewalk graffiti

the chalk makes one picture
a lemon by Braque
yellow and green
caked and distorted

the breaks in the walk
form another
a crooked web
of disintegrating concrete

the innocence of hopscotch
a mysterious semicircle
with contiguous squares
neatly numbered

and there, jeering in orange
underlined by a crack
Sheila sucks

feels like rain

Sitting on the back deck

this evening you can smell the testimony of salt,
pelagic anecdotes of iodine and kelp,
a southerly wind leaving its allusions in Halifax.

Cities don't enjoy hills, contrary to the myths
of Europe. Hills are country commoners.
Cities need the company of currents, harbors,

rivers. Water knows much and gossips cruelly,
broadcasting secrets of adultery and riots,
the shipping news, the song that draws you down.

Early summer

By the bursting poppies Evelyn,
twelve in the spring, flirts with a boy,
animated and inhibited
at the same time, a gust of confusion
on the road to enlightenment,
the wind shear that buffets the heart.
Roxy lies on the tiles in the shower,
legs straight out behind, the wilted
sprawl only a bitch can enjoy.
A bassoon plays five ascending notes
— *The little train* by Villa-Lobos —
radiating waves of desolation
through my inner chambers, emotions
shimmying like heat mirages.

Spectator

out in the grass near the corner flag
a boy kicks the ball in the wind

absorbed in the flight of this leather bauble
my mind is mute now vacant

I can feel my muscles soften and settle
fully immersed in a rising peace

scrabbling over the bald middle
the men keep it down on the ground

Equilibrium

Here's a deadlock, like the balance
between the zigzag of my upper teeth,
set in motion by a childhood knock,

and the crowding of the lower ones,
a gene from my dad. In our marriage
something similar has happened,

my faults familiar to you, yours to me,
this forbearance, learning to tolerate
and overlook, each needing something

from the other. The old theme — life adapting
to life. We've half raised our child now,
braces on her own near-perfect teeth.

Enlightenment

darkest is the dead of night
grounded sun beneath my feet
encircling personal eclipse

it's not true what people say
about the darkest hour
passing just before dawn

predawn is the morning penumbra
the horizon a low wattage glimmer
fraught with the idea of fire

About the author:

Ian Wiseman was born in Newfoundland in 1950, one year after Confederation, the only member of his family to be born in Canada. After growing up in the small mining and fishing town of St. Lawrence, he studied literature at Memorial University of Newfoundland and at Carleton University.

In 1968, while still in school, he began his professional career, writing for newspapers and magazines. In 1972, he became a television producer for the Canadian Broadcasting Corporation, where he would work intermittently until 1995. He won an Anik Award for documentary production in 1975.

From 1980 to 1995, he taught at the University of King's College in Halifax, Nova Scotia, where he still holds the honorary title of Inglis Professor. He was a visiting fellow at City University in London, England, in 1988-89, and a Maclean Hunter fellow at the Banff Centre for the Arts in Banff, Alberta, in 1993. He lives in Halifax with his wife, Nancy Robb, and their daughter, Evelyn.

Other books by Ian Wiseman:
Non-fiction: *A History of the End of the World.* Morrow, New York, 1982 (with Yuri Rubinsky)
Fiction, humor: *The Wankers' Guide to Canada.* Bantam-Seal, Toronto, 1985 (with Ian Brown, Marc Giacomelli, Robert MacDonald, and Yuri Rubinsky)